DIGGING UP THE PAST

TERRA-COTTA SOLDIERS
ARMY OF STONE

Arlan Dean

HIGH
interest
books

Children's Press®
A Division of Scholastic Inc.
New York / Toronto / London / Auckland / Sydney
Mexico City / New Delhi / Hong Kong
Danbury, Connecticut

Book Design: Mindy Liu and Jennifer Crilly
Contributing Editor: Geeta Sobha
Photo Credits: Cover and p. 1 © Ingo Jezierski/Getty Images; pp. 4, 21, 25, 41 © Keren Su/Corbis; pp. 7, 39 © Carl & Ann Purcell/Corbis; p. 8 © 2002 Geoatlas; p. 11 by permission of the British Library; p. 15 © Glen Allison/Getty Images, p. 16 © Lee White/Corbis; p. 19 © Greg Smith/Corbis; pp. 23, 34 © Lowell Georgia/Corbis; p. 26 The Art Archive/Bibliothéque Nationale Paris; p. 28 © Getty Images; p. 31 © Asian Art & Archaeology Inc./Corbis; pp. 32–33 © Joseph Sohm; ChomoSohm Inc./Corbis; p. 37 © O. Louis Mazzatenta/National Geographic Image Collection

Library of Congress Cataloging-in-Publication Data
Dean, Arlan.
    Terra-cotta soldiers : army of stone / Arlan Dean.
    p. cm. — (Digging up the past)
    Includes index.
    ISBN 0-516-25124-4 (lib. bdg.) — ISBN 0-516-25093-0 (pbk.)
    1. Qin shi huang, Emperor of China, 259–210 B.C.—Tomb—Juvenile literature. 2. Terra-cotta sculpture, Chinese-Qin-Han dynasties, 221 B.C.– 220 A.D.—Juvenile literature. 3. Shaanxi Sheng (China)—Antiquities— Juvenile literature.
    I. Title. II. Series: Digging up the past (Children's Press)

    DS747.9.C47D43 2005
    931'.04'092—dc22

                                                        2005002699

1 2 3 4 5 6 7 8 9 10 R 14 13 12 11 10 09 08 07 06 05

CONTENTS

This is the modern-day city of Xian (**shee**-onn). Nearby lies the tomb of Qin Shi Huangdi, China's first emperor.

Introduction

It is the year 1975. As you sit riding in the Jeep, you feel nervous and excited about your new expedition in China. You and your fellow archaeologists will be working on an incredible new discovery. It is an army of terra-cotta soldiers. Terra-cotta is a hard clay used in pottery and building construction. Finally, you reach your location and get out of the car. You quickly walk to the spot where farmers had dug and found the soldiers.

You peer into the large hole in the ground at the life-sized statues. You begin to recall many things you have read about this important archaeological discovery. You think about Emperor Qin Shi Huangdi, who ruled China two thousand years ago. The emperor used his army of real-life warriors to create a great dynasty. Today, it is the emperor's army of stone warriors that fascinates you. You cannot wait to work on digging out these cultural treasures!

Archaeologists are history's detectives, collecting clues from the past. They scientifically study human history through statues, tools, and other discoveries. They use their findings to understand how people in the past lived. The terra-cotta soldiers and the grave of Emperor Qin Shi Huangdi were exciting finds for archaeologists around the world. Although ancient historians wrote about Qin Shi Huangdi's empire, his tomb gave archaeologists evidence of the grand way of life of Qin Shi Huangdi.

This photograph, taken in 1983, shows one of the spots where digging for the terra-cotta soldiers took place.

Mongolia

China

Nort
Kore

● Peking

Great Wall

Yellow Sea

● Xian ● Xianyang

Yangtze River

East China S

The city Xianyang, which lies 12 miles (19 km) east of Xian, became the capital of the Ch'in empire. About 120,000 families were moved to Xianyang from various parts of China when Qin Shi Huangdi united China.

CHAPTER ONE

China's First Emperor

In central China, near the city of Xian, lies one of history's most important archaeological discoveries. In 1974, farmers who were digging a well discovered the tomb of Emperor Qin Shi Huangdi. Within four months of this discovery, archaeologists began to work on digging out the tomb. What they found was beyond their expectations. The tomb measured 20 square miles (50 square kilometers) and included almost eight thousand terra-cotta statues of soldiers and horses.

The statues represent Qin Shi Huangdi's army, which was known as the Ch'in army. This clay army was made over two thousand years ago. The terra-cotta soldiers were made and then placed in Qin Shi Huangdi's tomb to protect him in the afterlife. They were equipped with weapons, chariots, and horses that would enable them to guard the emperor's final resting place.

Emperor Qin Shi Huangdi

Before Qin Shi Huangdi (c. 259 B.C.–210 B.C.) became the emperor of China, he was called Chao Cheng. In 247 B.C., Chao Cheng was king of the state of Ch'in. Chao Cheng had become king when he was just thirteen years old. He considered himself greater than any ruler who had come before him. He created the powerful Ch'in army, which became famous for its many conquests.

At this time, China was divided into seven states. Each state had a different ruler. Under the command of Chao Cheng, the Ch'in army defeated the other six states. They conquered the land of China, state by state, until there was no one left to oppose them.

By 221 B.C., Chao Cheng united the seven states into one empire. He took the title Qin Shi Huangdi, which roughly means "the first emperor." The emperor created a powerful government to rule over his empire. He passed laws to standardize written languages, currencies, and weights and measures. These laws helped to build strong trade and business activities. A single written form of the Chinese language was created to keep the land unified.

Qin Shi Huangdi started to take tours of his united China in 200 B.C. The purpose of these tours was to make sure his plans were being carried out properly. But the emperor was also looking for magicians to help him live forever!

Qin Shi Huangdi had big plans for his empire. He ordered massive construction projects. He had huge palaces built throughout his lands. He also had roads built to connect the different parts of his empire. Large sections of the Great Wall of China were constructed under his command. Qin Shi Huangdi's tomb containing the terra-cotta soldiers, however, would prove to be the most important construction project to archaeologists.

ARTIFACT

The word *China* comes from the word *Ch'in*, which was the name of the state that Chao Cheng ruled.

The Emperor's Army

Emperor Qin Shi Huangdi's army was essential to creating and maintaining his empire. He trained his army to fight more effectively than his enemies' armies. The soldiers wore light armor made of leather. With less weight to burden them, they could move quickly and attack more forcefully. They used deadly weapons such as crossbows that shot arrows with poisoned tips.

THE WEAPONS OF THE TERRA-COTTA ARMY

Some of the weapons that were buried within Emperor Qin Shi Huangdi's tomb were well preserved and provide a glimpse of ancient Chinese warfare. The following are examples of the types of weapons used by the soldiers of the Ch'in army:

Gou: a long, curved, hooklike bronze weapon with blades on both sides

Jian: a bronze sword with a long, narrow blade

Mao: a spear that is 14 feet (4 meters) long

Nu: a crossbow used to shoot arrows over long distances

Pi: a 1-foot (0.3 m) sharp blade attached to a 10-foot (3 m) pole

Shu: a long, round bronze weapon that was used to show the authority of the soldiers holding the weapon

Much of Qin Shi Huangdi's army was made up of farmers who had been trained to fight. Sometimes men from wealthy families joined Qin Shi Huangdi's army. Joining the army was a way of showing loyalty to the emperor. Bravery and loyalty were very important to Qin Shi Huangdi. If a soldier brought back the head of an enemy, he was given money or a higher position in the army or government. Most of Qin Shi Huangdi's top officials were soldiers who had proven their intelligence and bravery in battle. The men that Qin Shi Huangdi promoted to government positions were very loyal to him.

Li Si

Qin Shi Huangdi's prime minister, Li Si, worked with him to bring about changes. Li Si began working with the emperor in 247 B.C. He remained prime minister until Qin Shi Huangdi's death in 210 B.C. Li Si developed a new standardized writing that is known as small seal script. He worked with Qin Shi Huangdi to break up China into separate regions. When the emperor died, Li Si was worried that the people of China would begin to turn against the government because the emperor was not a well-liked ruler. He kept the emperor's death a secret for about two months. Folklore says that Li Si would enter the emperor's royal carriage every day and pretend to have discussions with him.

The expression on the face of each terra-cotta soldier is different. Each face shows a different emotion. This official of Qin Shi Huangdi's government has a serious expression.

The soldiers of pit one (shown here) are arranged in a rectangle. Historians study the soldiers to find out battle plans of the victorious Ch'in army.

CHAPTER TWO

All the Emperor's Men

When the archaeologists began to dig out Emperor Qin Shi Huangdi's tomb, they found that it was very large and well decorated. It contained several features to keep the emperor safe and comfortable in the afterlife. The most impressive feature of the tomb was the terra-cotta soldiers.

Three pits were uncovered during the early years of digging. They cover a very large area that is about 215,278 square feet (20,000 sq. meters). Each of the three pits was skillfully built with thick walls of earth. The floors are paved with bricks. Within these pits is the terra-cotta army, accompanied by their horses. The terra-cotta soldiers were positioned facing the emperor's grave in order to guard it.

Learning From the Statues

There are about eight thousand terra-cotta statues. Since this army was to protect the emperor in the afterlife, careful attention was given to even the smallest detail of each figure. The statues represent different types of soldiers. Archaeologists and historians have determined that each statue was modeled after a real person.

Archaeologists studied the way the terra-cotta army was arranged in the pits. The soldiers were arranged in battle formation. The lineup revealed how the Ch'in soldiers fought so many wars successfully. The statues are posed as if in combat. For example, some bowmen stood with one leg in front of the other. One arm is drawn back, ready to shoot off an arrow. These bowmen would have fired their arrows from a distance. There are three ranks of bowmen. In battle, each rank would have taken turns firing. This plan was intended to produce a constant stream of arrows.

ARTIFACT

In Katy, Texas, a copy of the terra-cotta army is on display at an outdoor museum called Forbidden Gardens. These statues are much smaller than the original ones in China.

18

Shown here are the copies of the Ch'in terra-cotta soldiers that are the main attraction at Forbidden Gardens in Katy, Texas. There are six thousand terra-cotta soldiers in Forbidden Gardens' exhibit.

Pit One

The first pit that was dug out was the largest in the tomb. There are about six thousand terra-cotta soldiers in pit one. Most of the statues in pit one wear armor. There are over two hundred foot soldiers at the head of the army. The bowmen behind them wear knee-length jackets. In addition to the foot soldiers and bowmen, there are also spearmen in pit one. These spearmen, like the bowmen, did not wear heavy armor.

Also in pit one are thirty war chariots. Two of these chariots were command vehicles. These chariots were made of wood and fell apart over time. Four terra-cotta horses pull each chariot. There are one or two terra-cotta soldiers and a driver in each chariot. Officers sit atop two of the chariots. The officers wear special headgear and badges on their armor. The chariots were meant to protect the army. In battle, the officers riding the chariots would beat drums and ring bells. These noises signaled the troops to advance or to retreat while in battle.

Pit Two

Pit two holds about fourteen hundred statues. It is smaller than pit one. Like the statues in pit one, the figures in pit two represent bowmen, foot soldiers, and spearmen. In addition, soldiers on horseback are also in pit two. These soldiers are dressed in short armor. Two generals were found in pit two. Both wear special armor. A group of kneeling armored bowmen surround standing bowmen. These bowmen protected the rest of the army.

There are seventy chariots in pit two. Sixty-four of them were light chariots that had a driver and a soldier.

Archaeologists have been digging out and repairing the terra-cotta soldiers for over thirty years. This photograph shows the state in which the soldiers were found.

Like the chariots in pit one, these chariots were also made of wood and had rotted over time. They were used to protect the army from the sides. The other six chariots were large. In battle, soldiers on horseback would ride alongside these large chariots.

Pit Three

Pit three is the smallest of the three pits. There are sixty-eight terra-cotta statues in pit three. They are taller than those in pits one and two. Their large sizes were meant to show that they were important men. These statues represent army officers and other officials. There are four large chariots in this pit. They were inspection chariots. In battle these chariots would head out in front of the Ch'in army.

Warriors and Their Weapons

The terra-cotta soldiers were placed in the pits with real weapons. The weapons were made from bronze. Archaeologists have found over ten thousand weapons in the emperor's tomb. These weapons include real swords, daggers, spears, and axes. Scientists studied the metal content of the weapons.

Shown here is one of the arrows of the terra-cotta army. The arrows were made of iron and bronze. Some had tips made of lead.

The metals that were used to make these weapons show a great knowledge of metals for the time period.

More than six different types of armor have been found in the pits. All of the suits of armor are well designed. Archaeologists have been able to determine that the suits of armor were put on and taken off over the soldiers' heads.

DISAPPEARING PAINT

When archaeologists first dug up the terra-cotta soldiers, the colors of the paints were still visible. However, the colors began to fade quickly—sometimes within hours. This fading was due to the statues being in the open air for the first time in two thousand years!

The colors of this general's robes were originally dark purple and red. His pants were green and his shoes were black. The covering for his head was brown.

Qin Shi Huangdi had all books burned, except those that were on medical and scientific subjects. This painting shows books being burned and scholars being killed.

CHAPTER THREE

An Unfair Emperor

In the fifteen years of his rule, Emperor Qin Shi Huangdi made vast improvements to China. Despite these changes, Qin Shi Huangdi was not popular among his citizens. He taxed the people heavily and created very strict laws. The emperor severely punished or killed anyone who disagreed with him. His ambitions proved to be unfair to the people living under his rule.

Qin Shi Huangdi achieved his goals with a great deal of harshness. He drafted citizens from all parts of the empire to build his tomb. They were told that they had to be involved in building Qin Shi Huangdi's tomb in order to get to heaven. Prisoners of war were also put to work on building the tomb. The history records from that time show that over 700,000 people worked to build Qin Shi Huangdi's tomb.

The Burning of the Books

Qin Shi Huangdi was especially threatened by the ideas and teachings of Confucianism. Confucianism is a way of life that is based on the teachings of

Confucius is the first person who wanted to educate all men in China. His birthday, celebrated on September 28, is called Teachers' Day. This painting of Confucius was done around 525 B.C.

Confucius. Confucius was a teacher and philosopher who lived in the fifth and sixth centuries B.C. Confucianism is a set of beliefs that stresses social harmony, justice, and devotion to family ancestors.

Qin Shi Huangdi wanted the citizens of his empire to live strictly by his laws. Under Qin Shi Huangdi's rule, Confucianism became illegal. He believed that the ideas of Confucianism conflicted with the laws and the structure of his empire. He burned all books about Confucianism. Qin Shi Huangdi also had hundreds of Confucian scholars killed by burying them alive.

ARTIFACT

Qin Shi Huangdi was influenced by the writings of Han Feizi, who lived in China in the third century B.C. Han Feizi wrote that people are basically selfish and that rulers should reward their subjects for loyalty and severely punish them for disloyalty.

Forced to Serve

During Emperor Qin Shi Huangdi's time, most of the people in China were peasant farmers. Rich people took part of the food that the farmers grew as tax. In addition to working to raise food, the peasants were also forced to serve in the military. Also, Qin Shi Huangdi's great building projects took huge amounts of manpower. Men who would normally have been raising crops were forced to build the palaces, the walls, and the roads of Qin Shi Huangdi's empire.

The shortage of farm labor caused a drop in food production. Eventually, the peasant class was not able to provide enough food to feed itself. Hunger turned to anger, and the peasants soon turned against the empire they had helped to create. Shortly after Qin Shi Huangdi's death, the peasants rose up against the new emperor, Qin Shi Huangdi's son. They believed that he would cause them as much suffering as his father had. They looted and burned all the government buildings as well as Qin Shi Huangdi's great palaces. Because it was buried, only Qin Shi Huangdi's underground tomb with its terra-cotta army survived the uprising.

Since Qin Shi Huangdi banned art, there is almost no painting or drawing from the period of his rule. Everyday objects of that period, such as this cup, however, did survive.

THE GREAT WALL OF CHINA

The Great Wall started as a series of four walls that protected parts of China. It was completed during Qin Shi Huangdi's rule. However, the wall was reconstructed in later times. The wall that stands today was primarily built during the time of the Ming dynasty (1368–1644). The Great Wall is a series of walls and towers that are opened in certain spots. It was meant to keep out tribes of invaders from the north of China. The wall is over 4,100 miles (6,598 km) long. During Qin Shi Huangdi's rule, as many as 300,000 people worked on the wall. These people were soldiers, laborers, and convicts. Due to poor working conditions, such as extremely cold weather, many of these workers died.

The terra-cotta soldiers are carefully worked on in order to restore them to their original state.

CHAPTER FOUR

The Treasures of the Pits

In 1987, the United Nations Educational, Scientific and Cultural Organization (UNESCO) put Qin Shi Huangdi's tomb on its cultural heritage list. The purpose of this list is to protect sites, such as the tomb, that are important to history. People from all over the world visit the ancient site to get a glimpse of the life of an emperor in ancient China. Both archaeologists and visitors find the terra-cotta soldiers to be interesting evidence of the past.

Many archaeologists work to uncover the treasures of the emperor's tomb. The terra-cotta soldiers as well as all the other items within Qin Shi Huangdi's tomb provide solid information about the history of China. Along with ancient history books, the terra-cotta soldiers provide evidence of Emperor Qin Shi Huangdi's rule. Archaeologists are excited about the prospect of digging out the emperor's grave. To this day, Qin Shi Huangdi's grave has been left untouched.

Archaeologists will wait to work on the grave until they are sure that they can dig it out without disturbing the structure or the precious objects that lie inside.

MAKING THE STATUES

The terra-cotta statues are made from the heavy clay found in the area around Mount Li. This type of clay is strong enough to make large pieces of pottery. The upper parts of the soldiers, including their heads, are hollow. From the waist down, the statues are solid. Molds were used to form the different body parts, and then individual details were added to each piece. Each of the soldiers was originally painted with bright colors. Over time the colors have faded.

Qin Shi Huangdi's Tomb

Qin Shi Huangdi's tomb took thirty-six years to build. It was built in a manner that represented Qin Shi Huangdi's empire. Palaces, which no longer stand today, were built inside the tomb. His royal palace, towers, and government buildings were also re-created. After analyzing the soil of the tomb, archaeologists discovered that rivers and

This skull was found in pit two. It is believed to be the remains of a member of Qin Shi Huangdi's family.

seas of mercury were dug into the floor of the tomb. These rivers and seas of mercury represented the rivers and seas of China. The rivers were kept flowing by mechanical devices. The land of China, including its mountain ranges, was re-created on the floor of the tomb. On the ceiling above, the Sun, the Moon, and stars were painted to represent the heavens.

To protect Qin Shi Huangdi's tomb from grave robbers, mechanical crossbows were set up to shoot arrows at anyone who dared to break into the tomb. Then the men who set up the crossbows were buried in the tomb along with the emperor, since they alone knew how to avoid the deadly arrows. Women from Qin Shi Huangdi's court who did not have children were also buried alive in the tomb in order to provide the emperor with companions in his afterlife. Lamps, filled with special oil that would burn for a long time, were lighted before the tomb was sealed.

Qin Shi Huangdi's tomb was created to provide him in death with all the comforts that he enjoyed in life. The tomb was filled with precious jewels and objects. In other pits, statues of rare animals have been discovered. Qin Shi Huangdi was a hunter, and these statues represented the kinds of animals he liked to hunt. Household items, such as pottery and silk fabrics, were also buried in the tomb.

ARTIFACT

Yuan Zhongyi was one of the first archaeologists to start working on digging out Qin Shi Huangdi's tomb. In the beginning, he thought that digging out the tomb would only take one week. Archaeologists actually took three years to dig out the first pit!

Many people visit the site of Qin Shi Huangdi's tomb. Small versions of the terra-cotta soldiers are sold near the tomb as souvenirs for the tourists.

The Future of Qin's Tomb

Some of the terra-cotta soldiers were found in need of repair. Robbers who had broken into the tomb destroyed many of the soldiers. Today, work is being done to restore the terra-cotta soldiers to their original state. Shattered statues are being fixed and painted. All of the statues are being painted in their original bright colors.

In 2000, archaeologists discovered that fungus is eating away at the terra-cotta soldiers. They believe that visitors touching the soldiers may be one way that the fungus could have gotten on the soldiers.

They also believe that high temperatures have led to the mold growth. Steps were taken to develop a treatment for the mold.

Archaeologists hope that Qin Shi Huangdi's grave itself has remained untouched by grave robbers. They believe that countless priceless objects will be found in the emperor's grave. These items will tell us even more about ancient China and the Qin Shi Huangdi empire. Only time and the work of archaeologists will uncover what other wealth of information the tomb of Qin Shi Huangdi holds.

Shown here is Mount Lushan, the site of Qin Shi Huangdi's tomb.

New Words

ambitions (am-**bish**-uhnz) wishes to reach certain goals

ancestors (**an**-sess-turz) family members who lived a long time ago

archaeologists (ar-kee-**ol**-uh-jists) scientists who study the past by digging up old buildings and objects

artifact (**art**-uh-fakt) an object made or changed by human beings, especially a tool, weapon, or sculpture made long ago

Confucianism (kuhn-**fyoo**-shun-iz-um) a way of life that is based on the teachings of Confucius

conquered (**kong**-kurd) to have gained control of an enemy

dynasty (**dye**-nuh-stee) a series of rulers belonging to the same family

excavate (**ek**-skuh-vate) to dig into the earth to search for ancient remains

New Words

fungus (**fuhn**-guhss) a plantlike life form that has no leaves, flowers, or roots

looted (**loot**-uhd) to have robbed or stolen

mechanical (muh-**kan**-uh-kuhl) operated by machines

mercury (**mur**-kyuh-ree) a silvery, liquid metal

molds (**mohldz**) hollow containers that you can pour liquid into so that it sets in the shape of the containers

peasants (**pez**-uhnts) people who own small farms or work on a farm

promoted (pruh-**mote**-uhd) to have moved someone to a more important job

retreat (ri-**treet**) to move back from a difficult situation

revealed (ri-**veeld**) to have made something known

standardize (**stan**-durd-eyes) to use rules or models to make different things the same

For Further Reading

Allison, Amy. *Life in Ancient China*. Chicago: Lucent Books, 2000.

Lindesay, William. *The Terracotta Army of the First Emperor of China*. Corona, CA: Odyssey Publications, 1999.

O'Connor, Jane. *Emperor's Silent Army: Terracotta Warriors of Ancient China*. New York: Viking Children's Books, 2002.

Sherman, Josepha. *Your Travel Guide to Ancient China*. Minneapolis, MN: Lerner Publications, 2003.

Simpson, Judith. *Ancient China*. New York: Time-Life Books, 1999.

Resources

Organizations

Asia Society
725 Park Avenue
New York, NY 10021
www.asiasociety.org

The Field Museum
1400 South Lake Shore
Chicago, IL 60605
www.fieldmuseum.org

Smithsonian Institution
PO Box 37012
SI Building, Room 153, MRC 010
Washington, DC 20013-7012
(202) 633-1000
www.si.edu

Resources

Web Sites

Encarta: Great Wall

http://encarta.msn.com/encyclopedia_761569621/ Great_Wall_(China).html

This article from Encarta provides a detailed history of the Great Wall of China.

Travel China Guide: Museum of Qin Terra-cotta Warriors and Horses

www.travelchinaguide.com/attraction/shaanxi/ xian/terra_cotta_army/

Browse this site to view photos and read more information about the terra-cotta soldiers of Qin Shi Huangdi's tomb.

Xian History: The First Emperor of China

www.cnhomestay.com/city/terracotta/xian_history.htm

This Web site provides more history about Qin Shi Huangdi and his empire.

Index

Index

About the Author

Arlan Dean has written numerous books on a wide variety of historical nonfiction subjects. He currently works and lives in New York City.